Fiction Teacher's Book 4
Wendy Body

Series Editor: Wendy Body

Pearson Education Limited
Edinburgh Gate
Harlow
Essex
CM20 2JE
England and Associated Companies throughout the World

ISBN 0582 48840 0
First published 2001

Printed in Great Britain by Scotprint, Haddington
Designed by AMR, Bramley, Hants

The Publisher's policy is to use paper manufactured from sustainable forests.

Edinburgh Gate
Harlow, Essex

If you wish to enlarge any of the Shared Writing Examples for use in your teaching, you may do so.

Contents

Year 4 Fiction Summary Chart

Unit in Resource Book	Text Objective	Sentence Objective Links	Task
Term 1 Unit 1 A Story Set in the Past	**T10** to plan a story identifying the stages of its telling	**S2** to investigate verb tenses	Plan the stages of a story
Term 1 Unit 2 A Story Plan A story set in WW2	**T9** to use different ways of planning stories		Use different methods of story planning
Term 1 Unit 3 Writing Character Sketches	**T11** write character sketches focusing on small details to evoke sympathy or dislike	**S5** to practise using commas to mark grammatical boundaries	Write character sketches
Term 1 Unit 4 De More De Merrier For a Little Love	**T14** to write poems based on personal or imagined experience, linked to poems read	**S4** using adverbs with greater discrimination in own writing	Write poems linked to poems read
Term 1 Unit 5 A first draft ... what would you change?	**T12** to write ... linking own experiences to situations in historical stories	**S1** to re-read own writing to check for grammatical sense (coherence) and accuracy (agreement); to identify errors and to suggest alternative constructions	Check and write an historical story
Term 1 Unit 6 Paragraphs and Playscripts	**T15** to use paragraphs in story writing to organise and sequence narrative	**S5** to practise using commas to mark grammatical boundaries	Make a paragraph plan
Term 1 Unit 7 Paragraphs and Playscripts	**T13** to write playscripts, using known stories as basis	**S1** to re-read own writing to check etc (see Unit 5, above)	Write a playscript
Term 2 Unit 8 Describing Settings	**T10** to develop use of settings in own writing, making use of work on adjectives and figurative language	**S1** to revise and extend work on adjectives; link to work on expressive and figurative language	Describe settings
Term 2 Unit 9 A Fantasy Story For Younger Children ... (plot outline)	**T12** to collaborate to write stories in chapters, using plans with particular audiences in mind	**S2** to use the apostrophe accurately to mark possession	Write in chapters for a chosen audience
Term 2 Unit 10 Sea Timeless Song Song of the Railway Train	**T11** to write poetry based on structure and/or style of poems read		Write poems structured as poems read

Term 2 Unit 11 Using Descriptive, Expressive Language ...	**T13** to write own examples of descriptive expressive language based on those read. Link to work on adjectives and similes	**S1** to revise and extend work on adjectives; link to work on expressive and figurative language	Use descriptive language
Term 2 Unit 12 Using Descriptive, Expressive Language ...	**T2** to understand how settings influence events and incidents in stories and how they affect characters' behaviour		Understand the influence of settings
Term 2 Unit 13 Extract from Planet of the Robots	**T14** notemaking: to edit down sentence/ passage by deleting less important elements		Edit an extract to make notes
Term 2 Unit 14 Extract from Planet of the Robots	**T13** to write own examples of descriptive, expressive language based on those read	**S1** to revise and extend work on adjectives; link to work on expressive and figurative language	Describe characters
Term 3 Unit 15 A Choice of Endings!	**T12** to write an alternative ending for a known story and discuss how it would change reader's view of characters and events of the original story	**S2** to identify the common punctuation marks	Write alternative endings
Term 3 Unit 16 A Choice of Endings!	**T13** to write own longer stories in chapters from story plans	Revise Term 2 **S2** use of apostrophes	Write a longer story in chapters
Term 3 Unit 17 Write a Story in Chapters	**T11** to explore main issues of a story by writing a story about a dilemma and the issues it raises for the character		Write a story about a dilemma
Term 3 Unit 18 What do you think?	**T8** to write critically about an issue or dilemma raised in a story, explaining the problem, alternative courses of action and evaluating the writer's solution	**S4** The use of connectives ... to structure an argument	Write about issues in a story
Term 3 Unit 19 Hiker's Haikus A Celtic Blessing from Ireland	**T14** to write poems experimenting with different styles and structures, discuss if and why different forms are more suitable than others		Write poems in different styles
Term 3 Unit 20 Silver	**T15** to produce polished poetry through revision	**S2** to identify the common punctuation marks (semi-colons)	Revise own poems

Introduction

What Is Pelican Shared Writing?

Pelican Shared Writing is an easy-to-use resource for teaching shared writing. It comprises ten packs: one Fiction and one Non-Fiction pack for each year group for Years 2, 3, 4, 5 and 6. Each pack contains:
- one Writing Resource Book
- one Teacher's Book with copymasters
- a large sheet of acetate and a Pelican Page Clip

Each Writing Resource Book offers 20 units of work which cover all the NLS Writing Composition objectives for the year group. Each Writing Composition objective forms one unit of work. Links are also made to appropriate Sentence Level objectives.

Although *Pelican Shared Writing* stands alone, it has links to *Pelican Guided Reading and Writing* in terms of objectives and tasks and there are content links to *Pelican Big Books*.

The Writing Resource Books
- Each 48 page big book is split into three parts - one for each term's teaching objectives.
- Shared writing is rooted in shared reading, and so the Writing Resource Books contain the texts which not only provide the starting point for writing, but also act as models of the genre to be studied. Story plans and writing frames are sometimes included as well.
- There are quotes on and about the writing process from professional children's writers on the inside back cover of each Fiction Writing Resource Book. These are to initiate discussions on writing.
- The Non-Fiction Writing Resource Books have a summary of links to other areas of the curriculum on the inside back covers.
- Each book comes with a large sheet of acetate and a Pelican Page Clip for text marking and writing.

The Teacher's Books

The Teacher's Book in each pack contains:
- teaching pages for each Unit of work with detailed, step-by-step advice on what to do

for each shared writing session. There are also examples of completed activities which teachers can use to guide the class in composing a text. Units will usually take more than one shared writing session to complete.
- a small number of copymasters e.g. writing frames, character planners. These are for general use and can also be applied to other texts and writing activities
- copymaster versions of all the Writing Resource Book texts. These can be used to make overhead transparencies and in instances where it is helpful for children to have their own copy of a text e.g. for annotation.

Teaching Shared Writing

Pelican Shared Writing complements the National Literacy Strategy's *Grammar for Writing* guidance. *Pelican Shared Writing* concentrates on delivering the text level Writing Composition objectives whereas *Grammar for Writing* concentrates on sentence level objectives. *Pelican Shared Writing* adopts a similar approach to shared writing which may be summarised as follows:

Key Features of Shared Writing:
- Make explicit how purpose and audience determine form and style.
- Link the writing to specific objectives.
- Rehearse sentences orally before writing.
- Discuss and explain alternatives and choices.
- Keep rereading to maintain flow, meaning and consistency.
- Involve children in the revision and editing.

Shared Writing Techniques:

Teacher Demonstration

The teacher composes and writes, modelling for children how to compose a particular text type or tackle a writing activity. He/she thinks aloud; rehearses choices before writing; explains choices and makes changes. The children do not contribute to the composition but they are invited to offer opinions on, for example, the choice of words or sentence construction. Demonstration time will vary according to the nature of the text and children's competence, but avoid spending too long – the children need to try things for themselves.

Teacher Scribing

The teacher acts as scribe and builds on the initial demonstration by getting the children to make contributions to the composition or task. The teacher guides, focuses, explains and challenges the contributions e.g. *Why did you choose that word? That's a really good sentence construction because ....* While children could make their contributions orally by putting up their hands, it is preferable for them to use whiteboards (in pairs or individually) which ensures participation by all children. It is also advisable to take "Time Out" i.e. get children to turn to each other in pairs and discuss possibilities for 30 seconds or so.

Supported Composition

Supported composition is preparation for independent writing. Children compose a limited amount of text using whiteboards or notebooks – in pairs or individually. Their alternatives are reviewed and discussed and choices and changes made. Some differentiation can be achieved by seating children in their ability groups and asking one group to compose one sentence orally, another to write one or two sentences and a third to write several sentences. Supported composition will enable you to identify those children who will need to repeat or continue the task in guided writing i.e. those who need greater support.

Shared writing is the most powerful means of improving and developing children's writing skills. But they will not develop into proficient writers unless two things happen. Firstly they are given sufficient TIME to practise the skills and craft of writing for themselves, and secondly, they receive the FEEDBACK which will help them evaluate what they have done and so learn from it.

Teaching a Pelican Shared Writing Unit of work

Support for each step will be found on the teaching pages

Discussing the Text for each unit

- Introduce the task and the objective
- Read the text in the Resource Book with the class and discuss the content
- Draw out features of the genre

Shared Writing

- Demonstrate or model the particular features of the writing
- Scribe and guide the pupils' contributions
- Continue with supported composition by children working in pairs
- Check the children's learning

Independent Writing

- Children complete the writing task.
- They consolidate their learning by carrying out another similar task.

Checking the Objective

- Determine children's understanding of the objective and how far they can apply their knowledge by evaluating their writing.

Revisiting the Objective

- If needs be, repeat the whole process using the suggested activity.

Note: A Pelican Shared Writing CD-ROM is available for use alongside each year's work. For further details, please see the section on ICT, overleaf.

ICT and Pelican Shared Writing

ICT may be used by all pupils to support writing skills. The word processor or desktop publishing package can enable the child to focus on the development of ideas and the manipulation of the written word without the physical constraints imposed by the handwriting process. The ease of editing, the spell-checking facilities and the ability to move text around the page make ICT support programs valuable tools to include within the writing repertoire. Writing tasks offer the ideal opportunity to integrate and apply those ICT skills being developed in the ICT curriculum.

Almost any writing task may be approached using ICT as an optional writing tool. These writing tasks will offer strong links with the ICT curriculum, which aims for pupils to:

- 'develop their ability to apply their IT capability and ICT to support their use of language and communication'
- 'pass on ideas by communicating, presenting and exchanging information'
- 'develop language skills eg in systematic writing and in presenting their own ideas'
- 'be creative and persistent'
- 'recognise the strengths and limitations of ICT'

(QCA Scheme of Work for ICT, Aims and Purposes)

The 'Communicating' strand for ICT is inextricably linked with developing literacy. Computer access is a great resource for independent, group and class work, and is too valuable a tool to remain unused during the development of literacy skills. It is a great motivator and encourages collaborative work that can become more focused as children's attention is extended.

Within the suggested Year 4 Fiction Pelican Shared Writing activities, there are some clear links with Unit 4A 'Writing for Different Audiences', from the QCA Scheme of Work for ICT. Links to the most relevant National Curriculum Programme of Study objectives for ICT are listed in the table opposite.

The differentiated writing frames for Year 4 (Fiction and Non-Fiction) are available on the CD-ROM entitled Pelican Shared Writing Year 4 CD-ROM (ISBN 0582 50987 4), which can be easily installed on any machine supporting Microsoft Word. Here they may be adapted, should you so wish, to suit your particular needs. The CD-ROM also provides cross-referencing charts for both Writing and ICT targets, including the ICT Programme of Study references and links to the QCA Scheme of Work for ICT – collated and readily available for inclusion into planning records.

Year 4 Fiction
Relevant objectives from the ICT Programme of Study

Pupils should be taught:

1a

to talk about what information they need and how they can find and use it [*for example, searching the internet or a CD-ROM, using printed material, asking people*]

1b

how to prepare information for development using ICT, including selecting suitable sources, finding information, classifying it and checking it for accuracy [*for example, finding information from books or newspapers, creating a class database, classifying by characteristics and purposes, checking the spelling of names is consistent*]

1c

to interpret information , to check it is relevant and reasonable and to think about what might happen if there were any errors or omissions.

2a

how to develop and refine ideas by bringing together, organising and reorganising text, tables, images and sound as appropriate [*for example, desktop publishing, multimedia presentations*]

3a

how to share and exchange information in a variety of forms, including e-mail [*for example, displays, posters, animations, musical compositions*]

3b

to be sensitive to the needs of the audience and think carefully about the content and quality when communicating information [*for example, work for presentation to other pupils, writing for parents, publishing on the internet*].

4a

to review what they and others have done to help them develop their ideas

4b

to describe and talk about the effectiveness of their work with ICT, comparing it with other methods and considering the effect it has on others [*for example, the impact made by a desktop-published newsletter or poster*]

National Curriculum for England, ICT Programmes of Study

Writing Composition Objective:

T10: To plan a story identifying the stages of its telling

Links to Sentence/Word Level Work

S2: To investigate verb tenses

Text Copymasters: C4–9

Discussing the Text

- Read together 'A Story Set in the Past'.
- *What does the author use to tell us how Thomas came to be in this situation?* (Uses the device of a character remembering the past – a form of flashback.)
- Does the story remind children of anything? (It has overtones of 'Oliver Twist' which is a story they might know.)
- *What could happen next? How might the story end?*
- Points of style to discuss:
  - the choice of winter for the setting (evokes greater sympathy).
  - the way the character's name is not introduced immediately.
  - the building up of details about the characters.
  - the use of adverbs in the penultimate paragraph.
- Focus on verb tenses – especially irregular forms, e.g. sank.

Shared Writing: *this may take more than one session*

Teacher Demonstration

- Tell the children that you are going to make a plan of the first part of the story together and that you are going to do it in three sections: Opening, Flashback and Main Events.
- Ask them what happens in the first three paragraphs of the story and scribe the Opening summary as in the Shared Writing Example. Remind children that it is not necessary to write in full sentences when planning.

Teacher Scribing

- Write the Flashback heading.
- Ask the children what happens in paragraphs 4 and 5. Discuss and then scribe (see Shared Writing Example opposite.)
- Write the Main Events heading.
- Ask children what happens in paragraphs 6, 7 and 8. Discuss and then scribe (see Example.)
- Repeat for the final two paragraphs.
- At the top of a fresh sheet of paper write *The man catches Thomas.*

Supported Composition

- Reread the final paragraph in the book. *What clues are there here which suggest that the story might end happily?* ('kindly blue eyes' 'my young friend') Ask the children to discuss in pairs how they think the story might end.
- Discuss some of the suggestions. Take one, e.g. Thomas is adopted by the elderly gentleman. Write it at the bottom of the sheet of paper/board.

- *What we have to do now is to think how we are going to get from the point in the story where Thomas is caught to the end where he is adopted. What is the first thing that might happen?* Guide children to deciding that the elderly gentleman (ask for suggestions for a name) might ask Thomas why he is stealing. Write it down.
- Complete the remaining steps, e.g. Thomas explains what has happened to him; they take him home; he meets the rest of the family; as days go by they all get on well with each other; enquiries are made but no other relations are found.

Shared Writing Example:

OPENING

paragraphs 1–3

Set the scene: winter, starving Thomas begging on streets of London. People ignore him.

FLASHBACK

paragraphs 4–5

Thomas remembers how he came to London after both parents died. (Father killed in a farming accident, Thomas and mother homeless, mother becomes ill and dies.)

MAIN EVENTS

paragraphs 6–8

Thomas is desperate and starving so he decides to steal from a couple he sees in the street.

paragraphs 9–10

He tries to steal the woman's bag, but her father catches him.

Independent Writing
- Using the Shared Writing planning, children write their own ending to the story.
- Plan your own version of the story – changing the setting to the country, changing the characters and outcome, e.g. the main character is given a live-in job on a farm.

Checking Children's Learning
- *How did the planning help in writing your ending?*
- Have the children maintained tense consistency in their writing?
- Are the children able to identify the separate stages of the story in planning their own adaptation and not make great leaps towards a conclusion?

Revisiting the Objective
- Re-write (or annotate using the acetate) the last paragraph in the Resource Book (page 8) as follows: *The elderly gentleman's hand snatched his arm and spun him round. As Thomas looked up fearfully into a pair of cold grey eyes, he heard him say, "Not so fast, you wretched creature!"*
- Plan a different ending to the story.

Use different methods of story planning

Writing Composition Objective:

T9: To use different ways of planning stories

Text Copymasters: C10–11

Discussing the Text

- Read through the Story Plan together.
- *What is significant about the date mentioned in the setting?*
- *What does 'evacuated' mean?*
- This outline could make either a short story of two or three pages or a novel. Discuss how they would be different, e.g. the opening could be either one or two paragraphs or a complete chapter depending on the amount of detail that is given.

Shared Writing

Session 1

Teacher Demonstration

- Establish that the outline gives very little information about the characters – nothing about their appearances and personalities. There is also no real information about the setting. Tell the children that you are going to work on these features over the next two sessions.
- *We are going to start by looking at the character of John and I'm going to do this as a labelled diagram which could help us if we were going to write the story.* On a large sheet of paper, draw a 'stick' figure of a boy; write 'John, ten years old' underneath (see Shared Writing Example 1). *I think John would wear short grey trousers, long grey socks and lace-up shoes like lots of boys did in those days so I'll start the diagram off like this ...* Write appropriate labels.

Teacher Scribing

- *What else could we say about his clothes?* Select and scribe labels.
- *What about John himself? Is he tall, short, skinny, wiry, plump? What about his hair? His eyes and so on?* Select and scribe labels.
- *Let's think about what kind of person John is and what feelings he might have ...* Draw the big heart shape and write 'homesick, protective towards his sister'. *What else could I add here? Look through the outline ... does that help?* Select and scribe children's suggestions.
- *Is there anything else we could add to our notes about John?* (See Shared Writing Example 1).
- Complete the character diagram, read the labels and see if there is anything else children want to add.

Supported Composition

- Complete a similar character diagram for Susie with children working in pairs. Do this in four stages: physical appearance, clothes, feelings and general. Discuss, compare and select examples to scribe after each one.

Shared Writing Example:

1.

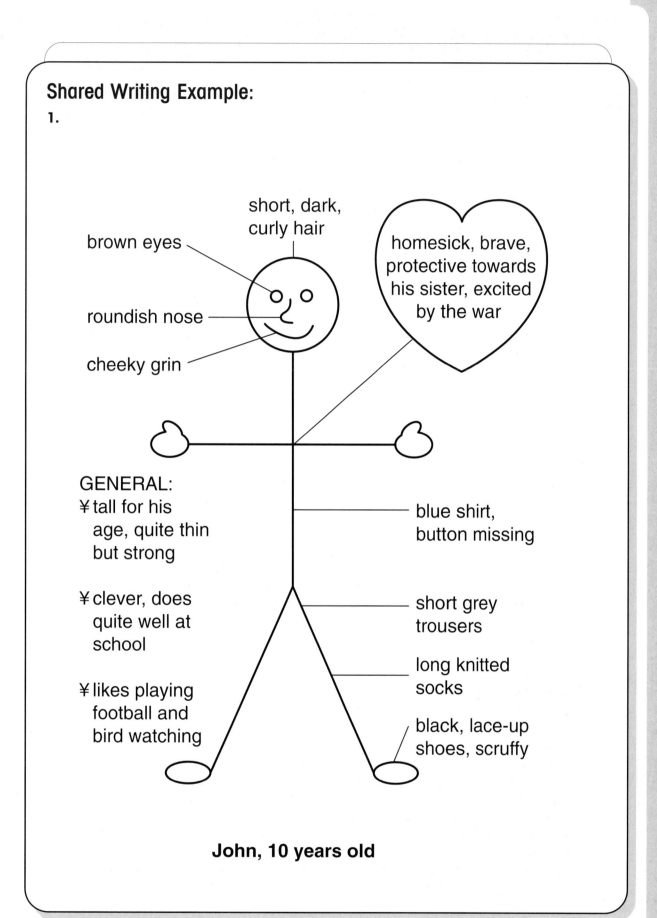

short, dark, curly hair

brown eyes

homesick, brave, protective towards his sister, excited by the war

roundish nose

cheeky grin

GENERAL:
¥ tall for his age, quite thin but strong

¥ clever, does quite well at school

¥ likes playing football and bird watching

blue shirt, button missing

short grey trousers

long knitted socks

black, lace-up shoes, scruffy

John, 10 years old

Independent Writing

• Children use either diagram to write a character description which could follow an opening sentence of: "I hate Miss Meechly!" said John as he was walking back through the wood with his sister, Susie.

Session 2
Teacher Demonstration

- Tell the children you are going to make two lists to help them draw a plan of the story setting. Write two headings as in Shared Writing Example 2.
- Look at the story outline in the Resource Book (page 8) and determine what is essential for the 'What we must have' list (see Example 2). Discuss each feature, e.g. *We need to think about where Miss Meechly's house is … is it actually in the village? No, because it says 'They run to the village and find Mrs Peters.'*

Teacher Scribing

- Take and scribe suggestions for the 'What we could have' list. *We need to think about the kinds of things you would find in a small village... it's in the country so what would probably be all around it? Yes, fields.*
- Read the lists and see if there is anything else children want to add.

Supported Composition

- *Work in pairs to help each other but each of you use your own whiteboards to draw a plan of the setting. First of all, put some woods right at the top of your board and write woods on it.* Demonstrate as in Shared Writing Example 3. Get the children to add Miss Meechly's house close to the woods and Mrs Peters' house as far away as possible.
- *Now I want you to plan the rest of the setting using the lists to help you.*
- Support as necessary then go through the completed plans, checking off the listed items.

Independent Writing

- Make a final version of the setting plan on paper.
- Children write the section of the story where John and Susie run to the village – using their setting plan to add detail and description. Ask them to decide if it is still dusk or a moonlit night before they start writing and what effect that would have on the setting.

Checking Children's Learning

- How successful were the children in creating a character diagram of Susie and the plan of the setting?
- How much use of their diagrams and plans did they make in their writing?
- Did they find (as is likely) that they planned more than they actually used in the writing?

Revisiting the Objective

- Create a character diagram for the German pilot.

NB Keep the work from this unit as it will be needed for Unit of work 3

Shared Writing Examples:

2. *What we must have*

a village

Miss Meechly's house (outside village)

Mrs Peters' house (other end of village)

somewhere for the pilot to land and then hide

a road

What we could have

fields around village

a wood

a school

a shop

a telephone box

a church

3. *A plan of the setting*

Write character sketches

Writing Composition Objective:

T11: Write character sketches, focusing on small details to evoke sympathy or dislike

Links to Sentence/Word Level Work:

S5: To practise using commas to mark grammatical boundaries

Text Copymasters: C12–13

Discussing the Text

- Look together at the illustrations of Miss Meechly and Mrs Peters from the WW2 Story Plan outline with which the children have been working.
- Discuss the illustrator's interpretations of the characters. Are they very different from how the children imagined them?
- Read the adjectives in the boxes and check that the children know what they all mean. Discuss how adjectives have been created from nouns and verbs, e.g. colourful, humourless, twinkling, giggly.
- Discuss how some of these adjectives make us feel towards the characters and whether they encourage us to like or dislike them.

Shared Writing:

Session 1
Teacher Scribing

- With the acetate clipped to page 10 for scribing, ask the children to suggest other words and phrases to describe Miss Meechly – both in terms of character and appearance. (See Shared Writing Example 1, opposite.)
- Read the list. Ask the children to identify the ones which suggest that Miss Meechly is not a pleasant character and underline them.

Teacher Demonstration

- Tell the children that you are all going to pretend that Miss Meechly has a twin sister who looks exactly like her but is the complete opposite in character. Write the heading as in Example 2. *We're going to write words and phrases to describe Miss Meechly's twin sister. I'll start you off. Instead of saying she has a <u>sharp</u> nose, I'll say she has a little pointed nose and she doesn't frown because she is bad-tempered but because she is short-sighted ...*

Supported Composition

- Ask the children to change the remaining underlined words so that they mean the opposite.
- Check and compare the children's suggested changes.
- Remind the children how writers use small details to make readers feel sympathy or dislike when they are describing their characters.

Independent Writing

- Children work in pairs to write a descriptive paragraph about Miss Meechly and a further paragraph about her twin sister. They should decide on first names for each of the sisters. Remind them about using commas to mark grammatical boundaries.

Shared Writing Examples:

1. **Miss Meechly:** <u>sharp nose</u>, <u>turned-down mouth</u>, dark-haired <u>frowning face</u>, <u>deceitful</u>, <u>unkind</u>, <u>unpatriotic</u>, <u>hard-eyed</u>, wearing a suit/jacket and skirt,

2. **Miss Meechly's twin sister:** a little pointed nose, frowns because she is short sighted, turned up mouth

3. **Mrs Peters:** Mrs Peters was plump and happy with a face that looked as if it was made for laughing with her twinkling blue eyes, dimpled cheeks and smiling mouth.

4. **Mrs Peters:** ~~Mrs Peters was plump and happy with~~ Plump and happy, Mrs Peters had a face that looked as if it was made for laughing with her twinkling blue eyes, dimpled cheeks and smiling mouth.

Session 2
Teacher Scribing

- With the acetate clipped to page 11, ask the children to suggest other words and phrases to describe Mrs Peters – both in terms of character and appearance.

Teacher Demonstration

- Tell the children that you are going to start them off on a description of Mrs Peters and write Shared Writing Example 3. Read it back, say you are not happy with the way it sounds and amend it as in Example 4. Point out the need for the comma after happy.

Supported Composition

- Children complete the description.

Independent Writing

- The children should now write the story outlined on pages 8 and 9 of the Resource Book (Text Copymasters C10 and C11). They should draw on both their work from this unit, and that completed in Unit of work 2 (character descriptions of John and Susie, information about the setting and the section of the story where John and Susie run to the village to find Mrs Peters).

Checking Children's Learning

- Do the children understand the concept of describing characters so as to produce feelings of sympathy/dislike in their readers?
- How far have they made use of the work on character and setting planning and descriptions in their stories?
- Is there evidence of use of commas to mark grammatical boundaries?

Revisiting the Objective

- Create and describe a twin sister for Mrs Peters, who is her opposite.

Writing Composition Objective:

T14: To write poems based on personal or imagined experience, linked to poems read

Links to Sentence/Word Level Work:

S4: Using adverbs with greater discrimination in own writing

Text Copymasters: C14–15

Discussing the Text

- Read together the two poems, 'De More De Merrier' and 'For A Little Love'.
- *What do the two poems have in common?* (Both in first person, neither use rhyme, both have lonely people looking for companionship or love.)
- *How do these poems make us feel?*

Shared Writing

Session 1
Teacher Demonstration

- Tell children that you are going to take the theme of loneliness and write two poems based on the examples in the book.
- *In the first poem, the girl is apart from everyone else but wanting to join them. I'm going to start us off with a similar situation. I need to remember to write in the first person and not to use punctuation – like the poet.* Scribe the first three lines of Shared Writing Example 1.

Teacher Scribing

- *What would the child be watching?* Take suggestions and scribe – it doesn't matter how many lines there are.
- *How long would the child be standing there alone in the playground? Till the end of playtime? Until the bell/whistle goes?* Take suggestions and scribe.
- *It's the end of playtime and so the child would go back into the classroom. How would she or he go – thankfully? slowly? sadly? What adverbs could we put here?* Take suggestions and scribe.
- Complete the poem in a couple of lines as per Shared Writing Example 1.
- Read the poem together.

Independent Writing

- Children write their own version of the poem. They can change as much as they wish but they must use different adverbs from the class version.

Session 2
Teacher Demonstration

- Reread 'For a Little Love'.
- Tell children that they are going to write a poem based on this but about friendship. *Imagine that you have no friends and what that must be like.*
- *Our poem is going to be about the things we would happily do or give for friendship.* Write the first two lines of Shared Writing Example 2.

Supported Composition

- *I want us to keep repeating 'I would …' but we can't use the same adverb each time. What could we use instead of 'gladly'?* Scribe a list of suggestions (see the rest of Example 2.)
- Ask children to select the first adverb and write the next line on their whiteboards. Compare and check.
- Repeat for as many lines as there are adverbs.
- Take some of the children's lines and share them with the class.

Shared Writing Examples:

1. standing in the
   playground noise
   watching all
   the others
   playing games
   until the bell
   when I go
   slowly
   sadly
   quietly
   back to
   our room

2. For a little friendship,
   I would gladly go to the end of the world.
   I would *happily* …
   I would *willingly* …
   I would *gratefully* …
   I would *cheerfully* …

Independent Writing

- Children write their own version of 'For a Little Friendship' using their own or other people's ideas from the Supported Composition.
- Prepare final versions for a class display or an assembly presentation.

Checking Children's Learning

- Were children able to use adverbs appropriately and effectively in their own poems?
- *Has writing these poems made you more aware of what it must be like to be alone and to have no friends?*

Revisiting the Objective

- Write a poem together called 'For a Little Peace' . This could be a serious poem about world peace or a humorous one – e.g. written by a teacher in a noisy classroom, or a parent at home.

Check and write an historical story

Writing Composition Objective:

T12: To write … linking own experiences to situations in historical stories

Links to Sentence/Word Level Work:

S1: To re-read own writing to check for grammatical sense (coherence) and accuracy (agreement); to identify errors and to suggest alternative constructions

Text Copymasters: C16–17

Discussing the Text

NB Use the shared reading and sentence work allocation of time for this.

- Tell the children that you are going to read the start of a story together. Explain that it is a first draft and there are quite a few mistakes which you will talk about as you go through.
- Read the text on Resource Book pages 14 and 15, identifying and discussing errors (see Shared Writing Example 1) e.g. *'She could hear the cow mooing as he waited to be milked.'* Cows are female so 'he' is wrong: *'She could hear the cow mooing as she waited to be milked.'* The trouble with that is that 'she' could refer to Mary! It would be better to say 'it' instead.
- Discuss the story: *How do we know it takes place a long time ago? What kind of character does Mary seem to be? What do you think Mary will do now? What would you do if you were in this situation?*
- Give out copies of Text Copymasters C16 and 17. Ask children to work in pairs to correct the mistakes you have discussed previously.
- Go through the corrections making sure that children have identified all the errors.

Shared Writing

Teacher Demonstration

- Remind children that this is a first draft and that although you have corrected the errors, there are other things that you could do to improve the writing. *We could change the order of things as well as changing the way some of the sentences are written.*
- *Let's start with the opening. I like the sentence about it being a Spring morning so I'm going to keep that but I think it would be better if we started off with it so I'm going to write …* (See Shared Writing Example 2.)
- *I also think it would be better if we had Mary thinking about the battle before she jumps off the gate to go and milk the cow. What do you think?*

Teacher Scribing

- *What shall I write? Are you happy with the way these three sentences about Mary's thoughts and feelings are written? How could we improve them?* Take suggestions, select and scribe – using Example 2 as a guide if necessary.
- Finish revising and rewriting the story opening. Read the revised version together.

Shared Writing Example:

1. Mary jumped off ~~of~~ the gate and lifted her long skirts to avoid the messy yard as she made her way to the barn. It was a bright Spring morning and the leaves ~~was~~ were just beginning to show on the ~~leaves~~ branches of the trees. She could hear the cow mooing as ~~he she~~ it waited to be milked. Mary couldn't help ~~but~~ feeling OR but ~~feeling~~ excited. She wondered if the battle would ~~of~~ have come any closer to their farm. She desperately wanted the ~~Kings'~~ King's men to win and ~~wishes~~ wished she could do something to help.

   She ~~pushes~~ pushed open the barn door and went inside. The cow was there as usual but so was something else ... It was one of the ~~Kings'~~ King's soldiers who ~~were~~ was wounded and sleeping.

2. It was a bright Spring morning and the leaves were just beginning to show on the branches of the trees. Mary couldn't help feeling excited – and a little scared – as she wondered if the nearby battle would come even closer to their farm. She desperately wanted the King's men to win and wished she could do something to help.

   The sound of the cow mooing broke into her thoughts. Mary jumped off the gate and, lifting her long skirts to avoid the messy yard, she made her way to the barn where Daisy was waiting to be milked.

   Mary pushed open the barn door and went inside. Then she gasped in surprise: Daisy was there as usual but so was someone else! Lying on the straw was one of the King's soldiers ... wounded and sleeping.

Supported Composition
- Ask the children to write the next two sentences on their whiteboards. *What do you think Mary will do now? What would YOU do if you were in this situation? How would YOU feel?*
- Invite the children to share and discuss some of their sentences and make a selection for scribing.
- Discuss how the story might end, writing notes if needs be, e.g. Soldier asks Mary for help – she gets water and food from the house – sees to the soldiers wound while he eats – he thanks her and says he needs to go back to the battle – she watches him leave, thankful that she has been able to help one of the King's men.

Independent Writing
- Children finish off the story: they should constantly ask themselves how they would feel or react and what they would do if they were Mary or the soldier.

Checking Children's Learning
- In groups, read the endings and discuss how well they work. Identify and correct errors. Identify and discuss how the writing might be improved.
- *How did 'putting yourself in someone else's shoes' help with your writing? Did it make it more 'real'?*

Revisiting the Objective
- Ask for a volunteer to have their work photocopied onto acetate to share with the class. Revise the writing.

Writing Composition Objective:

T15: To use paragraphs in story writing to organise and sequence narrative

Links to Sentence/Word Level Work:

S5: To practise using commas to mark grammatical boundaries

Text Copymasters: C18–19

Discussing the Text

- Tell the children that you are going to read the start of a story together and then plan the rest of the story. Point out that the story is not written in paragraphs.
- Read pages 16 and 17 together.
- *What clues are there in the story that tell us that it is not set in the present?* (names, governess, nursery at top of house, Papa's velvet slippers.)
- *Do you think the children's father is being unreasonable? Why?*
- *What do you think might happen next? How do you think the story might end?*
- Identify and discuss different uses of the comma, e.g. at the end of direct speech, marking grammatical boundaries in the first seven lines.
- Discuss where paragraph breaks might come in the text. Recap on how paragraphs mark a change of focus, time, place or speaker.

Shared Writing

Teacher Demonstration

- Tell the children you are going to start a paragraph plan for the story. Write 'Paragraph 1'. *I think the first paragraph break could come at the end of the sentence about the children being quiet and subdued … so I'm going to say that Paragraph 1 introduces the three children and the fact that they are unhappy.*
- Write 'Paragraph 2'. *I think that the next paragraph would end where it says that Papa had been unkind …* Write the summary sentence as in the Shared Writing Example.
- Write 'Paragraph 3'. The next paragraph could end at 'from the nursery'. Ask children what you could write for this summary.

Teacher Scribing

- Discuss and scribe the suggestions.
- Repeat for the remaining paragraphs of the text.
- Read the paragraph plan so far.

Supported Composition

- Discuss how the story might continue.
- Taking one paragraph at a time, ask children to use their whiteboards to write their suggestions as to what should be in each paragraph. Discuss, select and scribe as you go.
- Read the entire paragraph plan.

Shared Writing Example:

Paragraph 1 *(The nursery … quiet and subdued)*
Introduces the three children and the fact that they are unhappy.

Paragraph 2 *(Miss Jenkins … Papa had been so unkind?)*
The governess tries to cheer the children up but they don't want to do anything because their father has been "unkind".

Paragraph 3 *(Miss Jenkins … from the nursery)*
Explains that Papa finally became angry when the puppy chewed his new slippers.

Paragraph 4 *("But why … clutched Patch even tighter)*
Robbie and Maud are upset about getting rid of the puppy.

Paragraph 5 *(Daisy suddenly … would let Patch stay)*
Daisy says that if they buy Papa some new slippers he might let the puppy stay.

Paragraph 6 *(Miss Jenkins … under control in future")*
Miss Jenkins says that they will go and ask Papa and reminds the children how to behave.

Paragraph 7 *(Feeling a little … the wriggling Patch)*
They all go downstairs.

How the story could continue:
- They knock on Papa's study door, are invited in and Miss Jenkins explains that the children want to speak to their father.
- Daisy says how sorry they are and tells him that they will replace the slippers.
- Papa agrees but says the puppy cannot stay.
- Maud cries, Robbie and Daisy plead with their father, supported by Miss Jenkins.
- Papa weakens and changes his mind but extracts a promise that they will train the puppy and keep him in the nursery "away from me and my slippers!"

Independent Writing
- Children write the rest of the story using the paragraph plan. Remind them how paragraphs mark a change of focus, time, place or speaker and how they are separated by one line's space.
- Children share their work with a partner and check comma usage.

Checking Children's Learning
- How far have children understood the concept of paragraphing?
- Have they remembered the spacing between paragraphs?
- Have they used commas appropriately?

Revisiting the Objective
- Plan an alternative ending where Papa still refuses to allow the children to keep the puppy and another character, e.g. Mama or Grandmama, intercedes.

Write a playscript

Writing Composition Objective:

T13: To write playscripts, using known stories as basis

Links to Sentence/Word Level Work:

S1: To re-read own writing to check for grammatical sense (coherence) and accuracy (agreement); to identify errors and to suggest alternative constructions

Text Copymasters: C18–19

Discussing the Text

- Tell the children that you are going to turn the story about Daisy, Robbie and Maud into a play.
- Read pages 16 and 17 together, discussing and identifying direct speech, reported speech and where speech will need to be added.

Shared Writing

Teacher Demonstration

- *All plays have a Cast List – a list of people in the play and who they are. Write 'Cast List'. Who are the people in the story? List the names vertically. Now I need to say who they are. (See Shared Writing Example) I'm going to add a Narrator. The narrator or storyteller can describe or explain things which are difficult to get across in characters' speeches.*
- *The next thing we need is to say <u>where</u> the first part of our play is taking place so I'm going to write 'Scene 1: The children's nursery at the top of the house'.*
- *Now we can start to write what the cast or characters are saying. Look at the opening to the story … I think that this is where I need the narrator.*
- *When we are writing a play where do we put the name of the person who is speaking? I'm going to write 'Narrator' and leave a space before writing the speech. Remember, we don't use speech marks or 'said' in playscripts.*
- Write as in the Shared Writing Example.
- Continue with the rest of the speeches in the Shared Writing Example, pointing out that you:
  - are turning reported speech into direct speech and adding to it.
  - need to show *how* characters are speaking.
  - are adding stage directions for possible performance.

Teacher Scribing

- Read the final sentence on page 16. Write 'Miss Jenkins'. Ask children to discuss in pairs what she will be saying.
- Take suggestions, select and scribe.
- Read the first sentence on page 17. How can this be represented in the playscript? Is it a continuation of Miss Jenkins' speech? Is it spoken by the narrator? Or by one of the children? Ask children to discuss in pairs.
- Take suggestions, select and scribe.

Shared Writing Example:

Cast List   Daisy, a ten year old girl
                           Robbie, her eight year old brother
                           Maud, their six year old sister
                           Miss Jenkins, the children's governess
                           Papa, the children's rather stern father
                           Narrator

Scene 1
The children's nursery at the top of the house.

NARRATOR   The nursery at the top of the house was usually a fairly noisy and cheerful place, filled with the giggles and laughter of Daisy, her brother Robbie and sister Maud – but not today.

MISS JENKINS   *(brightly)* You are very quiet today, children; let's see if we can think of something to cheer you up. Shall I read you a story?

DAISY   No thank you, Miss Jenkins. I don't think we could concentrate on a story – not today.

MISS JENKINS   Well, what about going for a walk in the park?

ROBBIE   *(crossly)* We don't want to do ANYTHING. How can we go off and enjoy ourselves when Papa has been so unkind?

(Robbie goes to stare out of the window)

MAUD   *(crying)* I hate Papa!

Supported Composition
- Write Robbie's next speech. Scribe.
- Ask children to write the narrator's speech about Maud crying and clutching Patch. Discuss, select and scribe.
- Write Daisy's next speech. Discuss, select and scribe.

Independent Writing
- Children complete the playscript.
- Work in pairs to revise, checking for grammatical sense and accuracy, identifying any errors and suggesting alternative constructions. Also, see if stage directions can be added.

Checking Children's Learning
- Have children laid out their scripts appropriately?
- Can they define the functions of: a cast list, narrator, stage directions etc?
- How successful were they in the revision of their writing?

Revisiting the Objective
- Perform and check the playscript: six children should perform while the rest of the class use their whiteboards to take notes on how the speeches sound and where stage directions would help the characters to say their lines and make the action clearer for the audience.
- Revise the script accordingly.

Writing Composition Objective:

T10: To develop use of settings in own writing, making use of work on adjectives and figurative language

Links to Sentence/Word Level Work:

S1: To revise and extend work on adjectives; link to work on expressive and figurative language

Text Copymasters: C20–22

Discussing the Text

- Tell the children that they are going to read and extend descriptions of two different settings.
- Read together page 18, 'A strange planet'.
- Identify the adjectives and similes used in the description and discuss how effective the children think they are.
- Read together page 20, 'The hole in the hillside'.
- Identify the adjectives, simile and metaphors used in the description and their effectiveness in creating a picture in the reader's mind.

Shared Writing

Session 1
Teacher Demonstration

- Have the acetate clipped to page 19, which gives Suka's view. Reread page 18 ('A strange planet'). Then read page 19 together and tell the children you are going to extend this description.
- Say that you are going to annotate the page first of all and identify what you can add to the description. Mark the page as in Shared Writing Example 1.
- Add a sentence expanding on the general impressions of colour – see Shared Writing Example 2.

Teacher Scribing

- Change the comma after 'sky' to a full stop. *Now then, what can we say about the sky? Remember the watery green sun that was mentioned on page 18.*
- Take suggestions from the children – perhaps guiding them as in Shared Writing Example 3. Select and scribe.

Supported Composition

- Children write a sentence about the trees; remind them that this is a fantasy landscape and so they can let their imaginations run riot!
- Discuss, select and scribe.
- Children write a sentence about the rest of the scenery, selecting from the possible features you have written in the annotation.
- Discuss, select and scribe.
- Read the full, extended description.

Shared Writing Examples:

1.
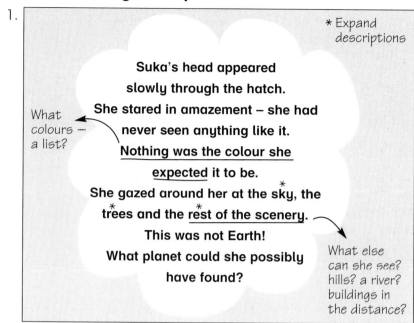

*Expand descriptions

What colours – a list?

Suka's head appeared slowly through the hatch. She stared in amazement – she had never seen anything like it. Nothing was the colour she expected it to be. She gazed around her at the sky, the trees and the rest of the scenery. This was not Earth! What planet could she possibly have found?

What else can she see? hills? a river? buildings in the distance?

2. It was as if the colours of half a rainbow had been wrapped around this world – blues, greens, violets and purples were everywhere.

3. A giant hand had painted it in different shades of pale green with touches of lilac and hints of purple.

Session 2
Teacher Scribing

- Reread page 20, 'The hole in the hillside', and discuss the illustration on page 21.
- List the following with big gaps in between for writing: Walls and roof of the cave; Lake; Treasure; Boat.
- Take suggestions for describing the walls and roof of the cave, e.g. studded with diamonds winking in the light from golden lanterns.
- Take suggestions for describing the lake, e.g. silent green depths

Supported Composition

- Ask the children to list their suggestions for describing the treasure on the banks of the lake. Scribe examples.
- Ask the children to list their suggestions for describing the boat. Scribe examples.
- Read what has been written – see if similes and metaphors could be added.

Independent Writing

- Leave the illustration and the above suggestions on view for children to write a complete description of what Marcus saw in the cave.
- Use Copymaster C1 to write own examples of descriptive language to depict a fantasy setting containing these elements.

Checking Children's Learning

- *What is the difference between a simile and a metaphor?*
- How effective are the children's choices of adjective?

Revisiting the Objective

- Make an overhead transparency of Copymaster C1 and complete with the class using a real rather than a fantasy setting.
- Select a child's completed example of Copymaster C1 and write a description from it.

Term 2 Unit of work 9:

Write in chapters for a chosen audience

Writing Composition Objective:

T12: To collaborate with others to write stories in chapters, using plans with particular audiences in mind

Links to Sentence/Word Level Work:

S2: To use the apostrophe accurately to mark possession

Text Copymasters: C23–24

Discussing the Text

- Tell the children that this is the plot outline for a story for younger children and then read the text on pages 22 and 23 together.
- *Which parts are outlined in some detail and which are very general?*
- *What do you think that Gran's news is likely to be?*
- *Do you think this story would appeal to children younger than you? Why?*
- *Does this story outline remind you of anything that you have read?* (e.g. *The Lion, The Witch and the Wardrobe*)
- Tell the children that this is to be a story in short chapters and discuss where chapter breaks might occur.

Shared Writing

Teacher Demonstration

- Using large sheets of paper, start the chapter plan. Explain that you are going to plan the story chapter by chapter and in each chapter you will note both the outline content and details which need to be included.
- *I think the first chapter should explain about Zara and how she discovers the old shed – with a cliff-hanger ending of her opening the door.* Write the Chapter 1 outline and details to include as per the Shared Writing Example. Comment on the use of apostrophes for possession.
- *Chapter 2 will finish when they walk through the shed wall. This is what I'm going to write for the Chapter 2 plan …* write as per the example. Again, comment on the use of apostrophes.

Teacher Scribing

- Ask children where they think the next chapter break might occur. (An animal begging for help?) This will make Chapter 3.
- *This part of the story is outlined very generally – we are only told that Zara is in a strange land with dwarves, gnomes and talking animals and that 'an animal' asks them for help. How could we flesh this out for our chapter plan?* Children should discuss possibilities in pairs for a minute before you take suggestions, select and scribe.
- What details will we need to include? Take suggestions, select and scribe.

Shared Writing Example:

CHAPTER 1:

Outline: Zara's mum is in hospital so Zara goes to stay with Gran. Explores Gran's garden, finds old shed and opens the door

Details to include: Descriptions of Zara and Gran; dialogue; description of garden

CHAPTER 2:

Outline: Zara goes in shed, finds table set for tea and friendly gnome waiting for her. They have tea, gnome says it's time to go, takes Zara's hand and they walk through shed wall

Details: Descriptions of shed and tea table; gnome's name and description; conversation asking about each other; Zara's feelings about walking through shed wall

Supported Composition

- *Chapter 4 covers the helping of the animal and Zara realising she must get back home to Gran. What help does the animal need? How will Zara and the gnome help?*
- Children should write outlines for Chapter 4.
- Compare outlines. Depending on their complexity, do any of them need more than one chapter? Select and scribe.
- Children should write outlines for the final chapter, Chapter 5, deciding on what the news is that Gran is waiting to pass on and whether or not Zara will tell her what has happened.
- Compare, select and scribe.

Independent Writing

- Remind the class that this is a story for younger children. Using the class chapter plan, pupils should write the story in their groups. Each group can write one given chapter collaboratively and then swap for checking and revision.

Checking Children's Learning

- Where children have used apostrophes in their writing have they done so correctly?
- Arrange for children to read the story to a younger class:
  - Did they enjoy the story?
  - Did they understand it?
  - Was the language use appropriate?

Revisiting the Objective

- Plan a sequel to the story in which Zara goes back to stay with Gran, meets the gnome again and they help a dwarf family whose youngest child is lost.

Write poems structured as poems read

> **Writing Composition Objective:**
> **T11**: To write poetry based on the structure and/or style of poems read

Text Copymaster: C25–26

Discussing the Text

- Read together the two poems, 'Sea Timeless Song' and 'Song of the Railway Train'.
- Do the children like the poems? Which poem do they prefer? Why?
- *What differences are there between the two poems?* (rhyme, use of imagery, repetition, punctuation).
- *Why does Grace Nichols repeat 'sea timeless'?* (to give a feeling of the sea going on and on?)

Shared Writing

Teacher Demonstration

- Tell children that you are going to write a poem based loosely on 'Sea Timeless Song' and that you have chosen to write it about Winter.
- Write the title: 'Winter Song'.
- *I'm going to start like Grace Nichols and write 'Winter come and winter go'. Sometimes winter is very wet and it seems to last for ages, so I'm going to write: 'Winter wet ... winter slow'. I'm going to repeat that like Grace Nichols does to show those wet winter days going on and on.* (See Shared Writing Example opposite).
- *Now I'm going to write about the icy winds and snow that we sometimes get in winter. I'll need a word to rhyme with 'snow' so I'll say that the winds toss and blow.* Write the second verse as in the Shared Writing Example.

Teacher Scribing

- *Let's list some words that will help you write the next verses. This is quite a useful thing to do when you are writing a poem which rhymes.* Ask for and then write words which rhyme with snow, e.g. flow, glow, show, grow, crow, low, fro.

Supported Composition

- Ask children, in pairs, to compose the next verse using the list of rhyming words to help them. *You could have something about hungry birds and winter crow or on freezing rivers skaters flow ... Whatever you write, remember that your verse must be the same structure as the ones I've written.*
- Ask children to read out some of their examples and then scribe two or three of the most effective.
- Read the complete poem all together.

Shared Writing Example:

Winter Song

Winter come
and winter go
Winter wet … winter slow
winter slow
winter slow
winter slow
winter slow

Icy winds
toss and blow
Winter wind … winter snow
winter snow
winter snow
winter snow
winter snow

Independent Writing

- *Write your own version of 'Winter Song'. You can include some of the lines we wrote together if you wish.*
- Using the Shared Writing version of 'Winter Song' as a model and starting point, children should work in pairs to write a poem called 'Summer Song' or 'Autumn Song'.

Checking Children's Learning

- Were children able to maintain consistency of form and structure in writing their own poems?
- Can they evaluate their own work, saying what they feel was successful and why, and what they found difficult and why?

Revisiting the Objective

- Reread 'Song of the Railway Train'. Together, write a poem in this style – about an aeroplane taking off or a modern train or ferry. For example:

You see the plane on the runway
The slow gathering of speed
Until it tears itself from the ground,
A mighty creature with silver wings,
It flies like a joyful bird.

Writing Composition Objective:

T13: To write own examples of descriptive, expressive language based on those read. Link to work on adjectives and similes

Links to Sentence/Word Level Work:

S1: To revise and extend work on adjectives; link to work on expressive and figurative language

Text Copymasters: C27–29

Discussing the Text

- Tell children that they are going to read the start of a sci-fi or space fantasy story.
- Read together the story about Zak and Della's encounter with a spacecraft.
- *Where does the story take place? Do you think the setting will change?*
- *What do you think might happen next?*
- *The title of this Unit of work is 'Using descriptive language …'. Do you think that the story has examples of this kind of writing?*
- Give children copies of Text Copymaster C27. Ask them to underline examples of descriptive, expressive language.
- Compare and discuss the children's underlining. Ask why they made their choices and how effective they think the chosen examples are.

Shared Writing

Teacher Demonstration

- Tell children that you are going show them an example of how to make a sentence more interesting by using descriptive, expressive language.
- *On moorlands you can often see groups of old rocks or boulders and Zak could well have seen some during his walk, so I'm going to write a sentence about that.* Write Shared Writing Example 1, opposite.
- *The sentence doesn't tell us that the rocks and boulders are old so I'm going to add something.* Write Example 2.
- *That is more interesting than the first sentence I wrote, but I can make it more expressive …* Write Example 3.
- Ask children to read the last sentence. *Why do you think I chose to write 'sleeping' and 'nestled'?* If it doesn't arise spontaneously, ask children whether you have used a simile or a metaphor.

Teacher Scribing

- Write Shared Writing Example 4.
- Ask children to discuss in pairs how the sentence might be improved.
- Take suggestions and scribe the better examples. Read them with the class and see if children have any thoughts as to if and how the sentences can be improved or expanded. Try to include examples of similes and metaphors and focus on particularly effective use of adjectives.

Shared Writing Examples:

1. Zak stopped to look at a group of rocks and boulders.

2. Zak stopped to look at a group of rocks and boulders which had been there for centuries.

3. Zak stopped to look at a group of rocks and boulders which had been sleeping for centuries nestled in the moorland turf.

4. Beyond the boulders was a stream.

5. As they walked, Della looked up at the clouds in the sky.

Supported Composition
- Write Shared Writing Example 5.
- Ask the children, either in pairs or individually, to expand and improve this sentence using either similes or metaphors along with adjectives. Fast finishers can write more than one version.
- Take suggestions and scribe the better examples. Read them with the class and see if children have any thoughts as to if and how the sentences can be further improved.

Independent Writing
- Children write a descriptive paragraph about the moorland, which brings together the elements of sky, rocks and stream along with anything they wish to include from the story text itself.
- Work should be shared and discussed within groups and any revisions made before descriptions are finalised.
- Display the work under a heading of 'Using descriptive language'.

Checking Children's Learning
- Do the children understand what is meant by descriptive, expressive language?
- Do they appreciate the difference between similes and metaphors?
- Are they able to use them in their own writing?

Revisiting the Objective
- Reread the text on Resource Book page 29 and discuss the illustration. Work with the class to expand the description of the 'enormous gleaming object', i.e. the spacecraft.

Understand the influence of settings

Writing Composition Objective:

T2: To understand how settings influence events and incidents in stories and how they affect characters' behaviour

Text Copymasters: C27–29

Discussing the Text

- Reread the story text with the children. Tell them they they are now going to plan and write the rest of the story.
- *Why is the story set in moorland?* (good place to have a walk and picnic and therefore get the characters to the action; lonely and deserted so (a) other people less likely to see spacecraft and (b) Zak and Della can't easily get help or run away and hide; there is space for the craft to land).
- *Could the story take place anywhere else as effectively?*
- *What do you think might happen next?*

Shared Writing

Teacher Demonstration

- Tell children that you are going to write some questions which will help to plan the rest of the story.
- Write the questions in the Shared Writing Example.
- Go through the questions and discuss possible answers and alternatives.

Supported Composition

- Give children copies of Copymaster C2, the Sci-Fi Story Planner.
- Ask them to fill in the first box.
- Take examples and share with the class. Tell children they can amend their own sheet if they prefer someone else's suggestion to their own.
- Repeat with the other boxes.

Independent Writing

- Children use their plans to write the story. Remind them about the use of expressive language and also the work they did in the last unit – which they could incorporate into their stories if they wish.
- Work should be shared and discussed within groups and any revisions made.
- Final versions of stories could be made into a class book.

Checking Children's Learning

- Do the children fully appreciate the reasons why the moorland setting is important to the start of the story?
- What evidence is there in the children's stories of descriptive, expressive writing?

Shared Writing Example: Sci-Fi Story Planner

Where is the spacecraft from?

e.g. a planet on the far side of the galaxy

Why has it come to Earth?

e.g. it was on a mission to learn about the inhabitants of other planets

What is special about it?

e.g. It has the power to make itself invisible to all or most people

---

Will the spacecraft land? *e.g. Yes*

Will aliens appear? *e.g. Yes*

What will they look like?

e.g. like hairless pale green humans with two brains

Are they friendly or hostile?

e.g. friendly – don't know how to be aggressive or violent

What do the aliens want [from Zak and Della]?

e.g. their time on any planet is limited so they want help to find one place that will tell them everything about Earth and humans

Will anyone [Zak and Della] go on board the spacecraft? What for? What will happen?

e.g. Yes, they are invited to look around it by the aliens

How will the story continue and end?

e.g. While they are looking round the spaceship Zak and Della suddenly think of a library as a place that will tell the aliens everything about Earth and humans. Four aliens disguise themselves and they and the children are transported to the local library. By touching each book, the aliens absorb all their contents. They all go back to the spacecraft and the aliens prepare to leave. They touch the children's foreheads and they fall into a deep sleep. The spacecraft leaves. The children wake and make their way home – having lost all memory of the spacecraft. "It's so peaceful here, nothing ever happens ..."

Revisiting the Objective

- Draw and complete the following chart:

Setting	How it influences characters
Fantasy/Sci-Fi	• *no need for Zak and Della to explain happenings to others*
Moorland	• *good place for aliens to choose to land* • *Zak and Della can't easily get help or run away and hide*
Library	• *obvious place to gain knowledge*

Writing Composition Objective:

T14: Notemaking: to edit down sentence/passage by deleting less important elements

Text Copymasters: C30–32

Discussing the Text

- Ask the children to identify the genre of the 'Planet of the Robots' extract from the title alone.
- Read the extract together.
- *What is the significance of the radio signals?*
- *Why do you think that the team weren't allowed to kill intelligent life?*
- Ask two or three children to give you a summary of the story.

Shared Writing

Teacher Demonstration

- Have the acetate clipped to page 30.
- Tell children that you are going to write a summary of this page. Ask them why being able to write summaries is useful (e.g. when reviewing a book).
- Explain that in order to write the summary you are going to edit down what is on the page. First of all you are going to underline what is essential.
- Underline the essential elements of the text as in Shared Writing Example 1, opposite. Comment as you go, e.g. *It's not really important that Sarah Few is reading the facts and figures from the computer; what's important is that the computer has detected radio signals in the first place – the facts and figures are just the evidence.*

Teacher Scribing

- Ask the children to read out the essential information you have underlined and list it as in Shared Writing Example 2.

Teacher Demonstration

- *Now I know exactly what has to go into my summary I can write it. What I have to do is to turn these notes and incomplete sentences into a connected piece with proper sentences.*
- Write Shared Writing Example 3. Refer to the list of points and comment as you write, e.g. *For my first sentence I'm going to say that it was the exploration team's mission to visit new planets because it explains exactly what they are doing and makes a good introduction … 'Ahead' doesn't make a lot of sense here so I'm going to say that they have just found the planet … I'm going to make the connection between the blue and green meaning there was life even stronger by using 'therefore' here … I'm going to start the final sentence like this: 'When the ship's computer detects radio signals,' – I need a comma there – and make the meaning very clear by saying that the radio signals prove there is not only life but also intelligent life.*
- Ask children to read the summary with you. Invite their comments.

Shared Writing Example:

1. The three members of the <u>exploration team</u> had <u>visited</u> hundreds of <u>new planets</u>. Not all of them were very exciting places, but <u>the green and blue planet</u> ahead of them <u>looked very special</u>. <u>Blue meant water and green meant plants.</u> This <u>planet had life</u>!

   Sarah Few was the mission leader, and captain of the exploration ship Spacerover 2. She was reading a series of facts and figures from Algy, <u>the ship's computer</u>.

   "Algy <u>can detect radio signals</u>."

   Jon Malone, the team's biologist, whistled in excitement. <u>"Intelligent life!"</u>

2. – exploration team visited new planets
   – green and blue planet ahead looked very special: blue meant water and green meant plants – planet had life
   – the ship's computer can detect radio signals – intelligent life

3. The exploration team's mission was to visit new planets. The green and blue planet they had just found looked very special because blue meant water and green meant plants. The planet must, therefore, have life on it. When the ship's computer detects radio signals, it proves there is not only life but also intelligent life on the planet.

Teacher Scribing

- Clean off the acetate and clip it to Resource Book page 31.
- Tell children that they are going to write their own summary of this page but that you will highlight the important information together first.
- Go through and underline what children think are the essential parts.

Supported Composition

- Ask children to transfer the underlined information into list form on their whiteboards.
- Sample the work and check that children have done the task correctly.

Independent Writing

- Children use the listed information on their whiteboards to write their own summaries.

Checking Children's Learning

- Ask for examples to be read out in the plenary session:
  - Have children written in full sentences?
  - Have they made changes or additions in constructing sentences?
  - Do the rest of the class think these are fair summaries of the content?

Revisiting the Objective

- Follow the same procedure using another story page from the Resource Book.

Writing Composition Objective:

T13: To write own examples of descriptive, expressive language based on those read

Links to Sentence/Word Level Work:

S1: To revise and extend work on adjectives; link to work on expressive and figurative language

Text Copymasters: C30–33

Discussing the Text

- *What does the text tell us about the characters?*
- *What extra information can we get from the illustrations on page 32? Can we tell which is Jon and which is Scott? Which one will be Scott?*
- *What can we guess about these characters?* (e.g. Scott and Jon are scientists; the humans are all intelligent and courageous – they have to be to do their jobs; they are probably enthusiastic; Algy is an advanced piece of technology; as leader, Sarah is probably a strong personality.)

Shared Writing

Teacher Scribing

- Clip the acetate to Resource Book page 33.
- Tell children that you are all going to think of words and phrases to describe the characters: *For example: we could say 'talking computer' in Algy's box or 'enthusiastic about his job' for Scott. Let's write down what the text tells us first of all.*
- Turn to page 30 and ask children what they can find about the characters there. Scribe.
- Repeat for page 31.
- Look at page 32. *What does the illustration tell us about each of the characters?* Encourage children to think of interesting and expressive adjectives and phrases. Scribe what the children say.
- *Now what can we infer or guess about these characters that I can write down?* Scribe what the children say.

Teacher Demonstration

- Read what has been written about Sarah Few. Can you add anything more? (See Shared Writing Example 1, opposite.)
- Tell children you are going to see if you can combine any of the adjectives or phrases. (See Shared Writing Example 2.)
- *Now I can use these phrases to write sentences describing her.* (Write Shared Writing Example 3.)
- Point out that when we are describing characters, we don't have to say everything about them all at once in one description. We can add details as we are writing the story. *For example, David Orme could have added details about Sarah like this on page 30* (write Shared Writing Example 4). *At the top of page 31 he could have said this* (write Shared Writing Example 5).

Shared Writing Example:

1. Sarah Few

   captain and leader; in her twenties, black; attractive; complicated hair style; wears a close-fitting purple uniform; doesn't wear jewellery; long slim neck and fingers; dark eyes; good at maths; intelligent and courageous

2. dark eyes shining with intelligence, complicated hair style swept back from her attractive face a young, black woman in a close-fitting purple uniform

3. Sarah Few was a young, black woman in a close-fitting purple uniform with a complicated hair style swept back from her attractive face.

4. She was reading a series of facts and figures from Algy, the ship's computer, her intelligent dark eyes shining with excitement.

5. "I suppose so," said Sarah and, pointing at the data with a long, slim finger, she added, "But there's something odd about it ..."

Supported Composition
- Ask children to read what has been written about Scott White and see if they can combine any adjectives or phrases as you did with Sarah.
- Take and discuss examples.
- *Now see if you can turn those phrases into sentences like I did.*
- Take and discuss examples.

Independent Writing
- Children choose one character and write a description from the notes made on page 33.
- Use Copymaster C3, Character Descriptions, to make notes on a character from a book currently being read. Combine adjectives and phrases from the notes into sentences and then write a description.

Checking Children's Learning
- How far are children able to make their choices of adjective both precise and interesting?
- How successfully can they combine adjectives and phrases and construct sentences?
- Do they understand that that characters do not always have to be described in one go?

Revisiting the Objective
- Repeat the Sarah Few teacher demonstration using the character of Jon Malone.

Writing Composition Objective:

T12: To write an alternative ending for a known story and discuss how this would change reader's view of characters and events of the original story

Links to Sentence/Word Level Work:

S2: To identify the common punctuation marks

Text Copymasters: C34–36

Discussing the Text

- Read together the story about Tanker.
- *The author of the story leaves readers to make up their own minds about how it ends and whether Tanker joins or resists the bullies. She is deliberately ambiguous – in other words the final sentence doesn't make it clear who is the friend and who is the enemy. Which do you think it is?*
- *What kind of boy is Tanker?* Discuss how this might be different depending on whether or not Tanker is a bully.

Shared Writing

Teacher Demonstration

- Recap on the two ways that the ending of the story could be interpreted.
- Tell the children that you are going to make a chart which not only gives the two endings and their implications but makes it easier to compare the two versions.
- Draw the chart in Shared Writing Example 1(opposite) and write the headings in the first column.

Teacher Scribing

- Ask the children what should go into each box and then scribe. Guide the children using the example if necessary.
- If it does not arise, point out that there are other alternatives to the "all good – all bad" scenario, i.e. Tanker could have been expelled from his old school as a troublemaker but now decides to change his ways and so resists joining the bullies, or he could have left his old school because his family moved and is so unhappy that he snatches at any offer of friendship – even from a gang of bullies.
- Read and discuss what has been written. Make sure children understand how the choice of ending changes the character of Tanker.

Supported Composition

- Ask children to decide which way they want the story to end and then write two or three sentences to add to the original which make the ending explicit.
- Share some of the sentences.
- Discuss whether or not these endings have implications for the rest of the story. Is there anything the children would change in the original story?

Shared Writing Example:

How the story ends	Tanker makes friends with the boy reading the comic	Tanker kicks the boy and tears up his comic
What could happen as a result	He will have to stand up to the gang of bullies but at least he is not alone	– there is no guarantee that the gang will make friends with him – he is likely to get into trouble
What kind of character is Tanker?	a strong character who stands up for what is right	a weak and cowardly character who is easily led by others
Why did Tanker leave his last school?	because his dad got a new job and so the family had to move	because he was expelled for bullying and causing trouble
Why was he given the nickname 'Tanker'?	because he wants to join the army and drive tanks when he leaves school	because he used to deliberately barge into smaller children and knock them over

Independent Writing

- Children write a review of the story which describes the two ways of interpreting the ending, the implications and their preference.
- Share work within groups:
  - discuss whether alternative endings, the implications and the writer's preference have been adequately covered.
  - identify the punctuation used and whether improvements could be made.
  - vote for one review per group to be shared with the rest of the class.

Checking Children's Learning

- Do children appreciate how the choice of ending influences the way we perceive Tanker? Have they made this clear in their reviews?
- Are children able to express their views coherently and give reasons for their statements?

Revisiting the Objective

- Discuss the implications if the boy reading the comic turns out to be the bully in the school and the gang are trying to get their own back on him. How does this alter our view of the other characters?

Term 3 Unit of work 16:

Write a longer story in chapters

Writing Composition Objective:

T13: To write own longer stories in chapters from story plans

Links to Sentence/Word Level Work:

Revise accurate use of apostrophes (Term 2, **S2**)

Text Copymasters: C34–36

Discussing the Text

- Recap on the story about Tanker.
- Give the children possible titles to consider: 'Tanker's Choice'; 'The Bully's Victim'; 'The Bullies' Victim'. What do they each imply? Which do children prefer? Discuss the use of the apostrophe of possession.
- *Could this story take place in real life?*

Shared Writing

Session 1
Teacher Demonstration

- Have Shared Writing Example 1 (opposite) ready to show to the children.
- Tell them that you are going to plan a longer version of this story about Tanker, who starts off as an unpleasant character but changes when he gets to his new school. Explain that you have already written the first part of Chapter 1 as a flashback.
- Read the example to the class.
- *Why have I called Chapter 1 'The Last Straw'? What does it mean?*
- Discuss the writing, the sentence construction, e.g. 'Tanker's mum began crying quietly as the Headteacher continued …' and the attitudes of each of the characters. *How well does Mrs Riley know her son?*

Teacher Scribing

- Tell the children that you are going to write the rest of Chapter 1.
- Use the questions below to guide the children and ask them what you could write. Discuss suggestions and then scribe.
- *What will Mr White say to Mrs Riley?* (e.g. Tanker has had enough chances and now he must be expelled)
- *Will he say anything to Tanker?* (e.g. he hopes he will be able to make a fresh start at a new school)
- *What will Tanker be thinking or feeling?* (e.g. shocked)
- *How are we going to show that this is a flashback?* (e.g. Tanker remembering the interview, bored at home waiting to go to a new school, missing his friends)
- *How shall we finish the chapter?* (e.g. Mrs Riley coming in and saying that she has found a new school on the other side of town and Tanker starts tomorrow.)
- Read the complete chapter. See if children can suggest any revisions or additions.

Shared Writing Example:

Chapter 1: The Last Straw

"I'm sorry, Mrs Riley, but Gerald has left us with no choice. His behaviour two days ago was the last straw and the governors and I have decided that he must be expelled."

Tanker's mum began crying quietly as the Headteacher continued, "We have tried everything with Gerald but he has refused to change his ways. He has already been suspended twice for bullying and the younger children are terrified of him."

Tanker knew this but he was pleased that his stupid headteacher knew it too.

His mates knew he was the top dog as well; they always joined in the laughs and encouraged him when he was showing those daft little kids who was the real boss of this school.

Mrs Riley looked at Mr White through her tears and said, "But Gerald's a good boy really – it's those friends of his who lead him astray. Please give him another chance."

Tanker knew Mr White would change his mind about expelling him. He was a right softie.

Session 2
Teacher Demonstration

- Write 'Chapter 2: The New School'. Tell the children that they are going to plan the chapter about Tanker's first day at the school together but you will start them off. Write: 'Tanker enters school gates with mum – his feelings and first impressions – what Mrs Riley says to him'.

Supported Composition

- Ask the children to write their suggestions for the rest of the chapter.
- Take suggestions, select and scribe (e.g. meets headteacher and what she says – taken to new classroom and introduced – how Tanker feels at break – remembering his old school – beginning to regret his behaviour? – responding to his mum's questions at the end of the day).
- Plan Chapter 3 in a similar way (e.g. two or three days later – Tanker is sent to work with a couple of young boys and listen to them reading – effect this has on him).
- Plan Chapter 4 – the 'invitation to bully' episode which Tanker rejects.
- Plan Chapter 5 – how Tanker and his new friend deal with the bullies.

Independent Writing

- Using the class chapter plan, written during the Supported Composition session, pupils write the story individually or in their groups. (Each group can write one given chapter collaboratively and then swap for checking and revision.)

Checking Children's Learning

- How far have children kept to the plan in their writing?

Revisiting the Objective

- Plan/write an alternative opening chapter in which Tanker has to move to a new school because his dad has been promoted to a job in a different town.

Writing Composition Objective:

T11: To explore main issues of a story by writing a story about a dilemma and the issues it raises for the character

Text Copymasters: C37–38

Discussing the Text

- Explain that this is the outline of a story about jealousy and the problems it causes, which the children are going to plan and write.
- Read the text together.
- Discuss the boy's actions – can the children understand why he acts as he does?
- How might both boys feel about what has happened?
- Would you, like his friend, have ignored what the boy did?
- Discuss possible answers to the two questions at the end of the text about what the boys will say to each other and how the story might end.
- Discuss where the chapter breaks might occur.

Shared Writing

Session 1
Teacher Scribing

- Explain that you need to agree on some information about the characters before you plan the story.
- Write the headings as in Shared Writing Example 1 (opposite). Ask for suggestions from the children, reach a consensus and scribe.

Teacher Demonstration

- Tell the children you are going to outline the first chapter for them. *I think the first chapter should introduce the two boys, tell us about their different circumstances and make it clear how strong their friendship is ….* Write the Chapter 1 outline in Shared Writing Example 2.
- Write the Chapter 2 outline in Shared Writing Example 2.
- Ask for children's comments on what you have written and amend your outlines if necessary.

Supported Composition

- Write outlines for the remaining chapters, with children working in pairs to write down their ideas. Discuss, select and scribe one chapter at a time. Use the rest of Shared Writing Example 2 to guide children if necessary.
- Read through the chapter plan. Make any changes/additions that the children think are necessary. You might want to add a general note to the effect that it will be important to show how the characters are feeling and their thoughts at key points.

Shared Writing Examples:

1.

	The boy	*His friend*
name and age		
appearance		
home-life		
Why they are friends:		

2. **Chapter 1:** introduces the two boys, emphasises their strong friendship, what they like doing together (could start with them doing something?) shows differences in their home circumstances

Chapter 2: the party invitation, what to do about a present (no money so makes something), arriving at the party, the entertainment, going out into the garden to play a game before tea, the boy starting to feel jealous

Chapter 3: boy looking at his friend's presents including his own home-made one, his thoughts, destruction of one present, father seeing and feeling sorry for him, boy's realisation of what he has done

Chapter 4: the father tells his son what his friend has done, asks him to think before doing anything, friend thinks, says nothing, they all have tea – boy feels more and more uncomfortable and ashamed

Chapter 5: everyone leaving, friend calls boy back and gives him one of his presents, boy confesses and apologises, friend says he understands and wants to share the presents his parents gave him, boy says can't share things because he has so little, friend says they share their friendship and that is the most important.

Session 2

Independent Writing – an extended session

- Read through the chapter plan.
- Suggest that a good way to start the story might be to have the boys outside somewhere – e.g. kicking a ball around, tracking each other in the park, playing commandos – perhaps starting off with two or three lines of dialogue.
- Children write the story.

Checking Children's Learning

- How well have the children interpreted the chapter plan?
- Have they made the reasons for character's actions clear?
- How well have they portrayed the friend's dilemma?

Revisiting the Objective

- Plan an alternative ending to the story where the friend confronts the boy over the destruction of his present. What would happen then?

Write about issues in a story

Resource Book
pages 42–45

Writing Composition Objective:

T8: To write critically about an issue or dilemma raised in a story, explaining the problem, alternative courses of action and evaluating the writer's solution

Links to Sentence/Word Level Work:

S4: The use of connectives ... to structure an argument

Text Copymasters: C39–42

Discussing the Text

- Read together the story on pages 42 to 45.
- Discuss what the story is about: is it about racial prejudice or something else?
- Explain that the main issue is how to deal with prejudice or harassment.
- Do the children assume that the main character telling the story is a boy? Why? Does it make a difference if it is a girl?
- *What does the phrase 'it was my eyes that were doing the talking' mean?* (See page 44).
- *We are not told what the storyteller says to the boy in the playground; what do you think was said?*
- *Do you think the storyteller is right to be confident at the end?*
- Discuss the choice of title: do the children appreciate that it is both a question to the reader and to the storyteller?
- What are children's general reactions to the story?

The Shared Writing

Teacher Demonstration

- Tell children that they are going to write critically about the issue raised in the story, explaining the problem, saying what the alternative courses of action might have been and evaluating the solution chosen by the writer for the main character. (Please point out that in works of fiction, writers are not necessarily representing their own views!)
- *First we need to say what the story is about ...* Write Shared Writing Example 1 (opposite).

Teacher Scribing

- *What else should I say about the story?* Take suggestions and scribe, amending if needs be in order to be concise.

Teacher Demonstration

- *Now we need to summarise how the main character deals with the problem before we think about what else he/she could have done, so I'm going to write ...* write Shared Writing Example 2.
- Ask children to discuss alternative courses of action in pairs and the reasons why they might or might not have worked.
- While they are in discussion, write Shared Writing Example 3 on a separate sheet of paper.

Supported Composition

- Tell the children that you want them to put what they have just been discussing into writing. Draw their attention to the words and phrases you have just written and explain that they might be useful in constructing their sentences.
- Discuss what the children have written, scribe examples using a variety of connectives.
- Read what has been written so far and then add Shared Writing Example 4 to the writing.
- Ask the children to write their opinions.
- Share some of the responses. How much consensus is there? Add the majority view to the writing.
- Read the writing through, pointing out and identifying the main sections.

Shared Writing Examples:

1. 'What Do You Think?' is about dealing with racial prejudice. In it, the storyteller confronts the boy who has been writing graffiti on the wall of his/her house …

2. The main character deals with the problem by threatening the boy responsible both physically and verbally.

3. However   Although   On the one hand
   On the other hand   Alternatively   Instead of

4. *Your opinion*

   In my opinion, therefore, the main character's solution to the problem was …

Independent Writing

- Children write their own version of the Shared Writing. Stress that their views and opinions may differ from those expressed in the class writing and that this is perfectly acceptable as long as they can justify what they say.

Checking Children's Learning

- Check that the following elements all present in children's writing: the issue raised in the story; explaining the problem in terms of saying what the story is about; considering what the alternative courses of action might have been and evaluating the main character's solution to the problem.

Revisiting the Objective

- Write in similar vein about the story featuring bullying on pages 34 to 39.

Writing Composition Objective:

T14: To write poems experimenting with different styles and structures, discuss if and why different forms are more suitable than others

Text Copymasters: C43–44

Discussing the Text:

- Read together 'Hiker's Haikus' on page 46.
- Establish the form of a haiku if the children are not already familiar with it, i.e. 17 syllables arranged in 3 lines of 5, 7 and 5. They do not have to rhyme.
- Discuss reactions to the poem and meanings of, for example: 'fuelled by bread and meat', 'incessant' and 'green scent no one could invent.'
- Read 'A Celtic Blessing from Ireland' on page 47.
- *Does the poem have a particular form? Might this be because it may not originally have been written in English?*

Shared Writing

Teacher Demonstration

- Tell the children that they are going to write their own linked haikus about things that dogs like.
- Write the title and first verse of Shared Writing Example 1 – 'A Dog's Life' (opposite).
- Ask the children if you have got the form right. Hopefully they will spot that there are 7 instead of 5 syllables in the last line. Amend as in the example.

Teacher Scribing

- Write the first two lines of the next verse in Shared Writing Example 1.
- Ask the children what you could write for the third line.
- Read the two verses.

Supported Composition

- Ask children to write the next verse, using the same structure and pattern. They could have a sleepy, happy, playful, thirsty dog – anything as long as there are two syllables in the adjective.
- Share their efforts and select and scribe two or three of the best.
- Write the first line of the last verse in Shared Writing Example 1. Ask the children to complete the final haiku to round the poem off. Guide them using the example if needs be.
- Read the complete poem.

Teacher Demonstration

- Reread together 'A Celtic Blessing' on page 47. Point out the first three lines starting with 'May', the fourth line continuing the third and the nature of the final lines.
- Tell children that they are going to write a blessing using the same number of lines and pattern and include the line 'And until we meet again,'. Suggest that not everyone worships the same God and so they might like to have 'May your God …' in the last line.

- *I'm going to start you off ...* Write the title and the first line of Shared Writing Example 2. You may like to read, but not write, the rest of the example to give children some ideas. Leave page 47 visible while they write.

Shared Writing Example

1. *A Dog's Life*
This is the best thing
That a friendly dog could have:
~~Lots of~~ Other dogs to meet.

This is the best thing
That a hungry dog could have:
Juicy bones to chew.

This is the best thing
That a sleepy dog could have:
A bed by the fire.

But the best of all
Is an owner who provides
Pats, strokes and cuddles!

2. *A Blessing*
May friends always smile at you,
May loneliness never find you,
May happiness always fill you
with joyfulness at living;
And until we meet again
May your God keep you safe and free from harm.

Independent Writing
- The children complete the blessing. Share and display their work or use in an assembly.
- Write your own linked haikus, e.g. about another animal.

Checking Children's Learning
- Can the children tell you the form of a haiku?
- Have they kept to the pattern of the original blessing in their own versions?

Revisiting the Objective
- Write haikus about the view from the window or the playground.
- Write a blessing for someone who is about to make a journey.

> **Writing Composition Objective:**
> **T15**: To produce polished poetry through revision
> **Links to Sentence/Word Level Work:**
> **S2**: To identify the common punctuation marks including ... semi-colons

Text Copymaster: C45

Discussing the Text

- Point out that this is an extract from the well-known poem which children have probably met before.
- Read the poem together and discuss its form – rhyming scheme and number of beats/syllables in a line.
- Discuss the use of personification.
- *What do you think about this poem? Do you like it?*
- *What do you think 'shoon', 'casements' and 'couched' mean?*
- Point out the poet's use of semi-colons and the use of the final ellipsis to show that it is an extract.

Shared Writing

Teacher Demonstration

- Have Shared Writing Example 1 (opposite) already written – with good spacing between lines to allow for changes.
- Tell the children that they are going to write a poem using the same pattern as Walter de la Mare used but the subject will be snow.
- Explain that today you want to focus on revising the writing to make the poems as polished and effective as possible. You are going to start off by revising some lines that you have already written.
- Read the first line of Shared Writing Example 1. *I'm happy with this because I want to keep the same structure as in the original poem.*
- Read the next line of Shared Writing Example 1. *I don't like this: snow falls very gently and 'dropping' sounds like something heavy so I'm going to say 'falls gently to the earth'. I think that 'earth' is better than 'ground' because it sounds softer.* Amend as in Shared Writing Example 2.
- Read from the beginning to the end of line 3 in Shared Writing Example 1. *That doesn't sound very good does it? Let's cross out that line.* Pause as if thinking. *'Sticks' isn't right, it sounds too harsh and it's not really what snow does ... I think 'covering' would be better so I'm going to write 'softly covering all the trees' for this line.*
- Read the next line of Shared Writing Example 1. *I don't like this either now that I read it again! You know what I haven't done? Walter de la Mare talked about the moon as if it were a woman and I haven't done that with the snow ... I think I want to create a picture of the snow as a woman reaching out and holding everything she sees – just like snow covers everything. 'Snow reaches out and holds everything she sees' would be too long so I'm going to use a word which means the same. I'm going to write 'The snow embraces all she sees;'...*
- Read all four lines together. Ask the children if they think your revised version is better than the first one and why.

Shared Writing Examples:

1. Slowly, silently now the snow
   Is dropping on the ground below;
   It sticks to the branches of the trees
   Snow flakes land wherever they please;

2. Slowly, silently now the snow
   falls gently to the earth below;
   ~~Is dropping on the ground below;~~
   softly covering all the trees
   ~~It sticks to the branches of the trees~~
   The snow embraces all she sees;
   ~~Snow flakes land wherever they please;~~

Independent Writing

- Tell the children that you want them to write their own poems about snow based on the form and structure of Walter de la Mare's poem. They can write four or six lines. *I want you to do a first draft just like I did and then we'll be working on revising and polishing up your poems later.*
- In a second session, ask the children to work in their groups to read, discuss and help to improve each other's work. The writer should say what he/she thinks about possible improvements before the rest of the group make suggestions (which the writer can reject!) Weaker groups will need more support from you during this session.
- Display draft and final versions of the children's work for everyone to see and compare. Have some of the children explain to the class why and how they made changes to their poems.

Checking Children's Learning

- Have the children kept to the right line length and rhyming scheme?
- Have they used personification?
- Is there real improvement between their first and final drafts?

Revisiting the Objective

- Select (with permission) one child's first draft. Work on revising it together.

Writing Descriptions of Settings

The Sky

The Light

Trees

Hills

Buildings in the distance

A River

A Cave

A Lake

Sci-Fi Story Planner

C2

Where is the spacecraft from? Why has it come to Earth? What is special about it?

Will the spacecraft land? Will aliens appear? What will they look like? Are they friendly or hostile?

What do the aliens want?

Will anyone go on board the spacecraft? What for? What will happen?

How will the story continue and end?

Name of the character	Information from the text	Information from the illustrations	What I can guess about the character

Sentence I can make from the notes which combine adjectives and phrases:

A description of the character:

A Story Set in the Past

Dusk was gathering as winter snowflakes drifted gently onto his ragged clothes.

"Spare us a copper, Mister!" he murmured, too cold, too weary and too hungry to raise his voice further.

"Get out of my way!" the rich, well-fed voice thundered in reply. The boy sank down onto the dirty pavement as the man pushed him aside.

Unit of work 1

Thomas, for that was his name, was in despair. Like other boys he saw on the streets of London, he was homeless and alone. He could not remember the last time he had eaten.

Unit of work 1

His dark matted hair fell forward over his pinched grubby face as he rested his head on thin trembling knees. His mind drifted as he remembered the past ... his strong laughing father, killed in an accident on the farm ... his gentle mother, weeping and terrified as they were turned out of their farmworker's cottage ... the long days on the road trying to find work and shelter.

Unit of work 1

The pictures in his mind changed. Thomas remembered how his mother had become ill and had finally died in his arms. He remembered his lonely trek towards London, hoping that there he would be able to find a life for himself.

Remembering: he was sick of remembering ... he had to do something.

The boy looked about him, rubbing the tears from his eyes. A little further along, a richly dressed young woman and her elderly father were looking into a shop window.

Thomas suddenly decided to do what he had so far refused to even consider doing. He was starving ... he had to have money for food.

Slowly and stealthily, Thomas crept up behind the couple. He stretched out a grimy shaking hand and grabbed the young woman's bag. Swiftly he turned, ready to lose himself in the side streets. But not swiftly enough.

The elderly gentleman's hand caught hold of his arm and spun him round. As Thomas looked up into a pair of kindly blue eyes, he heard him say, "Not so fast, my young friend!"

Wendy Body

Unit of work 1

A Story Plan

Setting:

A village in England in 1942

Main characters:

John: a ten-year-old who has been evacuated to the village

Susie: his eight-year-old sister

Miss Meechly: the middle-aged woman they live with

Mrs Peters: a forty-year-old woman who is a friend of the children

Opening:

John and Susie talking about how they hate living with Miss Meechly.

Pelican Shared Writing Fiction Teacher's Book Year 4 © Pearson Education Limited 2001

Main Events:

- They see a damaged German fighter plane and the pilot dropping by parachute.

- They try to find him but can't.

- That evening they are sent to bed but are woken by voices.

- Creeping downstairs, they discover Miss Meechly talking to the German pilot – in German.

- They run to the village and find Mrs Peters.

- Miss Meechly is arrested as a spy and the children go to live with Mrs Peters.

Writing Character Sketches

Miss Meechly

neat   severe   tweedy   greying   humourless

Unit of work 3

Mrs Peters

dimpled   colourful   vivid   twinkling   giggly

Unit of work 3

De More De Merrier

sitting on the

window-sill

looking down

on the street

watching folks go by

wanting

to be there

in the midst

of it all

but stuck up

here all by myself

no friend

no sister

no brother

not even a dog

to talk to

Opal Palmer Adisa

Unit of work 4

For A Little Love

For a little love,

I would go to the end of the world

I would go through ice,

but in my soul be forever May,

I would go through the storm,

but still hear the blackbird sing

I would go through the desert,

and have pearls of dew in my heart.

For a little love,

I would go to the end of the world,

Like the one,

who stands at the door and begs.

Jaroslav Vrchlicky (Czech Republic)
Translated from the Czech by Vera and
Andrew Fusek Peters

Unit of work 4

A First Draft: What Would You Change?

Mary jumped off of the gate and lifted her long skirts to avoid the messy yard as she made her way to the barn.

It was a bright Spring morning and the leaves was just beginning to show on the leaves of the trees. She could hear the cow mooing as he waited to be milked. Mary couldn't help but feeling excited. She wondered if the battle would of come any closer to their farm.

She desperately wanted the Kings' men to win and wishes she could do something to help.

Unit of work 5

She pushes open the barn door and went inside. The cow was there as usual but so was something else ... It was one of the Kings' soldiers who were wounded and sleeping.

Unit of work 5

Paragraphs and Playscripts

The nursery at the top of the house was usually a fairly noisy and cheerful place, filled with the giggles and laughter of Daisy, her brother Robbie and sister Maud. But not today. The children were very quiet and subdued. Miss Jenkins, their governess, had tried to cheer them up but had not succeeded. She had asked them what they wanted to do, did they want a story, did they want to go out for a walk? Daisy and the others had said that they didn't want to do anything. How could they when Papa had been so unkind? Miss Jenkins tried to explain that it was not surprising that Papa had finally got angry.

After all, in this latest piece of mischief, Patch had chewed up his new velvet slippers when he had escaped from the nursery. "But why do we have to get rid of him? He's only a puppy," Robbie cried. Maud just cried and clutched Patch even tighter. Daisy suddenly shouted that she had an idea. They could use their pocket money to buy Papa some new slippers and then perhaps he would let Patch stay. Miss Jenkins thought about it and then she smiled and said that they would go down to Papa and see what he said. "But remember, you must be very polite and promise to keep Patch under control in future." Feeling a little more hopeful, they all went downstairs – Maud trailing behind with the wriggling Patch.

Units of work 6 and 7

Describing Settings

1. A strange planet

The spacecraft landed like a damaged insect dropping awkwardly to the safety of a leaf. Clouds of dust and pebbles rose like angry bees disturbed in their hive until its surface was no longer as bright as a newly minted coin. It rested for a moment in the rays of the watery green sun and then the hatch slowly opened.

Unit of work 8

Suka's head appeared
slowly through the hatch.
She stared in amazement – she had
never seen anything like it.
Nothing was the colour she
expected it to be.
She gazed around her at the sky, the
trees and the rest of the scenery.
This was not Earth!
What planet could she possibly
have found?

Pelican Shared Writing Fiction Teacher's Book Year 4 © Pearson Education Limited 2001

2. The hole in the hillside

The hole in the hillside was waiting for them – waiting like the open mouth of a snoring giant. He could see the darkness beyond: black velvet, curled up and watching silently. The small creature took his hand and impatiently dragged him forward.

Stones reached out to trip him as Marcus stumbled into the entrance of the cave and was dragged on through the darkness.

"What do you think of THAT?" the creature cackled?

Pelican Shared Writing Fiction Teacher's Book Year 4 © Pearson Education Limited 2001

A Fantasy Story for Younger Children

Zara is a lonely little girl who goes to stay with her gran while her mum is in hospital. She discovers an old shed at the bottom of a very overgrown garden. Opening the door, she finds a table set for tea and a small friendly gnome waiting for her. After tea, the gnome says that it's time to go.

Unit of work 9

He takes her hand and they walk through the wall of the shed. Zara finds herself in a strange land with dwarves, gnomes and talking animals. An animal begs them for help. They manage to help the animal and then Zara realises she must get home to Gran. The gnome takes her back. Gran is waiting with news.

Sea Timeless Song

Hurricane come
and hurricane go
but sea ... sea timeless
sea timeless
sea timeless
sea timeless
sea timeless.
Hibiscus bloom
then dry-wither so
but sea ... sea timeless
sea timeless
sea timeless
sea timeless
sea timeless.
Tourist come
and tourist go
but sea ... sea timeless
sea timeless
sea timeless
sea timeless
sea timeless.

Grace Nichols

Song of the Railway Train

You see the smoke at Kapunda

The steam puffs regularly,

Showing quickly, it looks like frost,

It runs like running water,

It blows like a spouting whale.

Traditional Australian Aboriginal poem
translated by George Taplin

Unit of work 10

Using Descriptive, Expressive Language

Zak sprawled against the ancient weathered stones with the sun warming his face like the flames of a welcoming fire.

First had come the walk across the moorland and then the picnic. Now he and his older sister, Della, were resting, half-awake, half-asleep and ready to dream. Della slipped into sleep and Zak could hear her gentle snores mixing with the busy sound of bees among the heather.

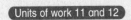
Units of work 11 and 12

The humming and buzzing got louder and louder – almost as if his ears were filled with bees. He sat up and gasped.

"Della! Wake up!" he screeched wildly.

Della's heart pounded. She felt as if some giant hand had knocked every breath from her body.

Units of work 11 and 12

In front of their terrified gaze, about a hundred metres away, an enormous gleaming object was hanging in the air – a huge spinning bauble that filled them with fear.

Wendy Body

Units of work 11 and 12

Planet of the Robots

The three members of the exploration team had visited hundreds of new planets. Not all of them were very exciting places, but the green and blue planet ahead of them looked very special. Blue meant water and green meant plants. This planet had life!

Sarah Few was the mission leader, and captain of the exploration ship Spacerover 2. She was reading a series of facts and figures from Algy, the ship's computer.

"Algy can detect radio signals."

Jon Malone, the team's biologist, whistled in excitement. "Intelligent life!"

Pelican Shared Writing Fiction Teacher's Book Year 4 © Pearson Education Limited 2001

"I suppose so," said Sarah, "but there's something odd about it. There's no speech. Just machine codes, computer data, that sort of thing."

"Sounds like an advanced civilisation to me," said Scott White. He was the expedition's geologist. He loved poking around amongst rocks. No planet was boring for Scott.

Sarah decided to land in a quiet place on the night side of the planet, just in case the locals were unfriendly. The team could defend themselves, but they weren't allowed to kill intelligent life on any planet.

Pelican Shared Writing Fiction Teacher's Book Year 4 © Pearson Education Limited 2001

Sarah set the computer to automatic landing. Algy found a quiet valley. Soon the ship was safely down.

from *Planet of the Robots* by David Orme

Units of work 13 and 14

Character Adjectives and Descriptions

Sarah Few

Algy

Jon Malone

Scott White

Unit of work 14

A Choice Of Endings

Tanker swung the heels of his shoes against the wall while he waited for the bell to ring. Watching, but not seen to be watching, the bustle of children at play around him, pretending that he didn't care that he was all alone. He hated this school.

"Make friends," his mum had said. Huh! What did she know? He'd never wanted to move. He'd never wanted to leave the old friends who had given him his nickname and filled his days with laughter and companionship.

Pelican Shared Writing Fiction Teacher's Book Year 4 © Pearson Education Limited 2001

"Oi!" said a voice. "We been watching you. D'you wanna join our gang?" Tanker's heart leapt in hope but he didn't show it.

"Yeah," he said, looking at the tall thin boy who had asked the question. "I might as well."

"O.K.," the boy replied. "But you gotta do something to prove you're one of us. See that kid over there with his nose stuck in a comic?"

Tanker nodded slowly.

"Get over there, give him a kick and rip up his comic."

Pelican Shared Writing Fiction Teacher's Book Year 4 © Pearson Education Limited 2001

"Why?" asked Tanker.

"Cos it's my gang and I said so!" grinned the tall thin boy.

Tanker mooched slowly across the playground, praying that the bell would go. It didn't.

He went up to the boy reading a comic and said, "Hey, you!" It was as simple and as difficult as that.

Now he'd made a new friend ... and a new enemy.

Wendy Body

Writing a Story in Chapters

The main character is a boy with two brothers. Mum left when the children were small and Dad has struggled to bring them up alone. The boy has a best friend – an only child with well-off parents. At his friend's birthday party, the boy suddenly starts to feel jealous. While everyone is out in the garden, he slips indoors and destroys one of his friend's many birthday presents.

Unit of work 17

Unknown to him, the friend's father sees the boy and hears his jealous outburst. He takes his son to one side and tells him about it. As everyone is leaving, the friend calls the boy back and gives him one of his gifts. The boy is ashamed and tells his friend what he has done.

What will they say to each other now? How will the story end?

Unit of work 17

Pelican Shared Writing Fiction Teacher's Book Year 4 © Pearson Education Limited 2001

What Do You Think?

As I went through the gate, Gramps was just putting the finishing touches to the wall at the side of our house. It looked all fresh and clean again ... not like this morning.

I remembered what it had looked like when I had left for school. Words that had made me feel sick to read them, words screaming out hatred in bright red paint.

Unit of work 18

I'd known, yes I'd known immediately who had done it. I'd known who'd hated us enough to share their hatred with any passer-by. But I had made sure that it wouldn't happen again.

I smiled as I watched my grandfather cleaning his brushes and remembered what had happened that afternoon.

Unit of work 18

I hadn't said a word to the boy all day; it was my eyes that were doing the talking. Finally, I had gone up to him in the playground and before he could say a word I had grabbed him by the neck. I had spoken to him – loudly enough for everyone else to hear. My anger had made me strong. My pride had made me fierce. He hadn't known this new me, but he'd recognised that I was now the strong one and that he was now the victim ...

"Hallo, Gramps," I said cheerfully. "You've made a great job of that wall."

He rubbed his back and then replied, "Well it's all right as long as they don't come back tonight. What do you think?"

"Don't worry, Gramps." I said confidently. "It won't be happening again."

Wendy Body

Hiker's Haikus

i
This is the best way
To travel: on your two feet
Fuelled by bread and meat.

ii
On footpaths, through fields
Of daisies, cowslips, clear streams,
Alone with your dreams.

iii
Far from motorway's
Incessant roar, dust and stink –
Slow steps, time to think.

iv
Inhaling pure air
Seasoned with birdsong, green scent
No one could invent.

v
Quiet happiness,
Moving thoughtful, calm and slow;
The best way to go.

Vernon Scannell

Unit of work 19

A Celtic Blessing from Ireland

May the road rise to meet you,

May the wind be always at your back,

May the sun shine warm on your face,

The rain fall softly on your fields;

And until we meet again,

May God hold you in the palm of

his hand.

Traditional Irish

Unit of work 19

Silver

Slowly, silently now the moon

Walks the night in her silver shoon;

This way, and that, she peers, and sees

Silver fruit upon silver trees;

One by one the casements catch

Her beams beneath the silvery thatch;

Couched in his kennel, like a log,

With paws of silver sleeps the dog ...

Walter de la Mare

Unit of work 20